The Wisdom of a Cloud

The Wisdom of a Cloud
A Book of Poetry

Parker Bradley

The Wisdom of a Cloud: A Book of Poetry

Copyright © 2023 by Parker Bradley

All rights reserved. No part of this book may be scanned, uploaded, reproduced, distributed, or transmitted in any form or by any means whatsoever without written permission from the author, except in the case of brief quotations embodied in critical articles and reviews. Purchase only authorized electronic editions and do not participate in or encourage electronic piracy of copyrighted materials. Thank you for supporting the author's rights.

Cover design: copyright © 2023 JRR Designs

Published 2023 Parker Bradley
Printed in the United States of America

ISBN: 979-889034443-4

Illustrations by Matthew Walden

Table of Contents

Beneath the Golden Bough

A Spring's Lesson for the Christian

Moldovan Moon

Afternoon Sun

Boyish Blue

The Wisdom of a Cloud

The Devil's Pawn

The Butterfly

The Watchman

Mother's Hands

Beneath the Golden Bough

When I first moved to Tennessee I rented a small place in Nashville that was still on pastureland but was near the city. It was a pleasant place to walk and enjoy nature. One of the largest maple trees I have ever seen grew out on a hillside and was a brilliant color in the Fall. The tree was later toppled and the land developed, but the memories of the place still remain and are treasures to me.

Beneath the Golden Bough

I took a walk through autumn woods
On paths through ages worn,
With silent lips and praying heart
A peace was in me born.

A scampering squirrel to winter's storehouse
In twilight glow I found,
Climbing upwards, upwards climbing
Into the Golden Bough.

Warbling wren and distant crow
Were forest's only sound,
Save for the drifting yellow leaves
That spun towards the ground.

When there an angel did appear,
Her look solemn though proud,
Did raise her eyes to speak to me
From 'neath the shining bough.

"Two hundred years of toil," said she,
"By farmer, mule, and plow
With gentle hand have touched this land
That lies beneath you now."

A look of smiling memory
Was there upon her brow,
When she, ending her reverie,
Rose into the Golden Bough.

A moment passed in soft reflection
Treasured to me now,
But fast the setting sun retreated
Through orange painted cloud.

The lowing herd was gathering,
Their heads did raise and bow,
Birds nestled ' neath a downy wing
High in the Golden Bough.

I turned my head toward hilltop lights,
To home, and there did vow
To ne'er forget the moment met
Beneath the Golden Bough.

That forest now is memory
For men have through it torn,
But the angel's voice will not retreat
Nor the peace then in me born.

—October 2001

A Spring's Lesson for the Christian

While home sick one day I took a walk on a warm winter's afternoon and saw a small stream flowing down a neighbor's hillside, carving its way through a difficult path. Nothing could stop that little stream from continuing on. It inspired me.

A Spring's Lesson for the Christian

This strange warm winter's afternoon
I walked a nearby dell,
And learned a thing from a fresh spring
And learned it very well.

He wasn't but a tiny stream
Not half an arm's length wide
And flowing from his distant home
Beneath my own hillside.

Winding here and stumbling there
He sought his 'termined end,
Smiling round each corner's turn
And laughing round each bend.

Some simple people sometime past
In ignorance or wrath
Spewed waste unwanted or unloved
Into his merry path.

He flowed between a radiator
Covered up with weeds
That stretched their sprouting shoots above
To Sun where'er it leads.

He fell over a buried tire
And past a purple bike
With streamers on the handlebars,
Once joy to long grown tyke.

Right past machine now rusted, left
By careless blinded men,
And through the roots of Ironwood tree
His strength was never dimmed.

Undammed, ungovernable and unmatched!
Inspiring was to see
His ever steady journey to
Some glad bright shining sea!

—*January 2, 2004*

Moldovan Moon

On a mission trip to the small Eastern European country of Moldova to assist orphanages there, I was moved by the experiences these orphans shared and the history that country has endured. I awoke late that night at our team house and penned this poem in a single sitting. The hope of Jesus penetrated even the hardest of places.

Moldovan Moon

The evening sky
Is a sunflower hue,
And the old woman sets
A small table for two.
The old man is passed
By a child on the path
Who skips as she sings:
She doesn't know wrath.
And the Moldovan moon
Chases day from the sky,
And says to bless God
For the night draweth nigh.

I went to a place
Where children are left
Who found themselves orphans
Or just couldn't be kept.
And they wandered about
Through the concrete and cold
In their hearts they were young,
In their eyes they were old.
And a dove cooed a song
In the branch overhead,
And said "These are not dead,
No, these are not dead."

The old farmer lay
On his old cotton bed
Recalling spent sweat
And the blood that was shed.
The old woman sits
In her chair in the night
And mourns for the dark
And prays for the light.
But the Moldovan moon
Pools the rows as it shines
And says, "Dawn is nearby,
Yes, the dawn is nearby."

The creases are cut
In their faces from birth
From their powerful burdens
All their days on the earth.
The orphans of chance
Tucked away past the wall
Just hoping for someone
To look at them all.
But they are not forgot
Says the words of all time
For He says, "You are Mine,"
For He says, "You are Mine."

And the Moldovan moon
Disappears in the dawn,
In a sky turned to sapphire,
Amethyst and then bronze.
The old farmer looks out
With a tear down his face.
"Bless God", says the woman
And sighs in His grace,
While the barefooted child
Plucks a flower and says,
"I am not dead,
No, I am not dead."

—*May 2008*

Afternoon Sun

When my mom relocated to Nashville,
I would go by on Sundays and spend the afternoon
there watching the hours go happily by. Her sun room window
opened to the west and the setting sun would filter through a
towering maple tree and fill the room with welcome light.
It was a wonderful place to find solace and rest.

Afternoon Sun

I had a cheerful friend to come
And visit me today,
Who filled the room with happiness
Without a word to say.

At times with great encouragement,
At others sweet repose,
In such delightful company
We watched the hours grow.
Until the fall of evening time
The sun did take its leave,
And bid me kind, "Farewell
Until tomorrow, if you please."

—April 2019

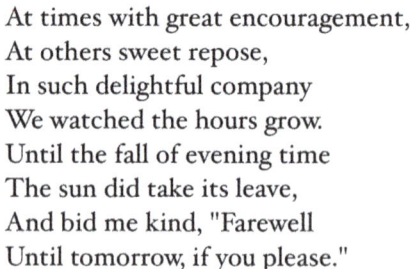

Boyish Blue

No matter what age a man may grow to achieve,
every now and then you can catch a laugh,
an expression, or spontaneity that gives a hint
to what he was like as a carefree boy. Especially
when my dad is cutting up around his closest friends,
I see little hints of his boyishness like sky peeking through
a blanket of clouds, the boy still there in the gray-haired man.
This celebrates how special my dad is to me and to so many.

Boyish Blue

I saw a patch of boyish blue shine through
A sky of silver, white, and gray,
And it made me glad not far beneath the billows
Lay the sky's most favorite hue.

A starry flash and golden beam betray the wrinkled line;
Even a fleeting glimpse is enough
To outlast and to recall the boyish blue
That runs underneath and goes on past time—
Forever.

—*January 2008*

The Wisdom of a Cloud

The second half of this poem came before the first. With lots of questions about where life was heading and not knowing what to pray, I looked up while sitting outdoors and saw a wisp of a cloud spinning and drifting lightly overhead. It brought me out of my heaviness and reminded me of the joy we have as followers of Christ and helped me regain perspective.

The Wisdom of a Cloud

Beneath an early summer sky
I walked alone through fresh mown fields,
My mind beset with puzzling doubt
At grinding work and meager yields.

My hope was dwindling in the dust,
I raised my swirling laden head
And caught a cloud as it danced by
And smiling this is what it said.

You are free
Free as me
Be not bound
By earthly ground
Rise renewed
To skies of blue
Awash in sun
With shadows none
Perspective high
To stretch the eye
Light as air
Above all care
Drift atop
The breaths of God
The winds that blow
He alone doth know
You are free
Free as me
Be not bound
By earthly ground.

—*June 2022*

The Devil's Pawn

This poem is a contemplation
on how easy it is to slip into sinful habits small and
great that rob the Christian of fellowship and freedom.
We befriend easy words and make excuses too easily,
abandoning the riches of God's grace and returning
to the chains Christ broke away in His victory.
We may know the way, but will we walk in it?

The Devil's Pawn

I cannot move, I cannot smile,
Just strain against the unseen chains,
All fastened by familiar hands,
To squeeze the courage from my veins.

Useless, helpless, wrestling on,
Struggle becomes identity,
Accustomed to the discontent
That is my only company.

Knowing strength and choosing weakness,
Now I truly understand,
Rebellion, even subtle,
Can so undermine a man.

So why not pray and why avoid Him
Who would then destroy the dark?
I have befriended easy words
And rendered powerless my heart.

Unconfused and ever knowing
Christ, this is the hardest fact,
So taught the Way to golden Day,
Yet satisfied to never act.

—*May 2004*

The Butterfly

My stepmom died in a tragic auto accident that took her from so many that loved her dearly. Though her life was marked with tragedy, she encouraged thousands as a teacher and friend. She always loved butterflies and saw them as a symbol of resurrection. What a legacy of faith and friendship she left behind.

The Butterfly

The Butterfly was born
Amidst tragedy and grief,
Her cocoon wrapped around
To shield and bring peace,
People spoke as they smiled
As her colors did show,
How lovely, how lovely
She grows, she grows
How lovely, how lovely she grows.

Her wings pressed against
The cocoon tightly bound,
But still her bright colors
Touched the world all around,
And people proclaimed
Both from near and afar,
"What a blessing, a blessing
You are, you are,
What a blessing, a blessing you are."

'Til one day in a moment
She broke suddenly free,
Her wings now stretched ready
For her prepared journey,
Then she blazed up to heaven
And a welcoming sky,
I love you, I love you,
Goodbye, goodbye,
I love you, I love you,
Goodbye.

—*November 2022*

The Watchman

I wrote this after my best friend brought his second daughter into the world. We talked about how afraid he was to raise children in the world as it is today and how he had nightmares about it. He turned out to be a really great dad raising four happy kids. Still, we prayed for them often, and he was always a watchman for them—
like all dads are, I suppose.

The Watchman

Darkness, Darkness
Now is moving
Rolling on its tidal way
Fading, fading
Is the fire
That burns so bright on glorious day.

Winging, winging
Little birds
That dive into the barren top
Whooing, whooing
Is the owl
Whose hunting eye does never stop.

Calling, calling
Are the calves
Now distant from their mother's side
Glowing, glowing
Are the eyes
Of creatures that in thicket hide.

Children, children
Run to home!
Stay safe behind your shuttered pane
Sleeping, sleeping
Warm in bed
'Till sun does shine his light again.

Watching, watching
Is the man
Who stands in strength against the night
Guarding, guarding
Precious ones
Whose dreams are sweet and breaths are light.

Rising, rising
Is the star
That signals the approach of morn
Waking, waking
Is the world
That sounds of voices free from harm.

—*October 2003*

Mother's Hands

I wanted to write a poem celebrating my mom.
The title was in my head for a long time, because of all
the things she has done for us and for so many all her life.
It all flowed out a couple weeks before Mother's Day.
It's a celebration of all Moms as well, what they mean to us,
and the good that their hands can do in this world.

Mother's Hands

Mother's hands are trained by Heaven
In the work of Providence,
Having in them the gifts of sandwich making
And cookie baking to lift the spirit
And gladden the heart of a child between backyard adventures,
Yet also the old man musing on life,
Greedily counting each grain in the hourglass.

Mother's hands are without time,
Arranging the colors of Creation in snatches of Eden,
Collected in vases to brighten the eye of the most downcast soul,
Then laboring on technology caught in her palms
To cheer the child and encourage the friend.

They are engines for the son and the daughter
On the field of play or in the disciplines of youth,
Cheering and clapping their efforts and strivings,
Each child pushed along by the single voice
Among the noise of thousands that has lifted its blessing
Since first breath was taken in a wearying world.

They are kept ready and supple, undaunted and eager,
By the scented lotions of magnolia bloom, orange peel,
And apple flower applied in brief moments of rest,
Swirling in memories of days long past,
When grandchildren gathered around her feet in the salty beach air
And the sun glinted upon a turquoise sea.

Her hands pass beyond the world of sight
As hymns of faith rise from each stroke of the piano key,
Indwelling the air and illuminating more than afternoon sun
    could touch,
Angels pausing on their missions of mercy to hear
The melodies and be glad that with them
Goes a faith that would challenge lions.

Mother's hands are made by the God of all comfort,
His vessels of blessing to remind the world that He is near,
Beacons in the dark to terrify devils
As they fold in prayer or raise in triumphal expectancy,
And they shall go on, beyond the days they are given,
For they have shaped the greening world and
    shared with it beauty unvanquished.

—*May 2022*

www.ingramcontent.com/pod-product-compliance
Lightning Source LLC
Chambersburg PA
CBHW042029050526
44107CB00104B/818